OVERCOMING FEAR

BY

PASTOR DENNIS LEONARD

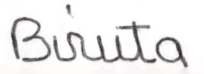

> I would like to thank my **entire** staff. Their faithful love and support has helped bring this book to God's people.
>
> I would especially like to thank Mark Grasmick, Linda McFann and Liz Hewitt for their dedication to this project.
>
> **Pastor Dennis Leonard**

All rights reserved.
Dennis Leonard Publications

Copyright © 1992
by Dennis Leonard Publications
1301 South Clinton
Denver, Colorado 80231
(303) 369-8514

Contents

1. Worry Is Nothing More Than Fear 9

2. Peace In The Middle Of The Storm 19

3. Be Careful What You Say 31

4. Fear Of The Future 39

5. How To Overcome Specific Fears 45

6. God Is My Refuge 53

Introduction

For even when we came into Macedonia our flesh had no rest, but we were afflicted on every side: conflicts without, fears within. **II Corinthians 7:5**

We all have fears, even the great apostle Paul had fears. Paul knew that fear would paralyze the church of Corinth and would keep them from accomplishing God's plan in their lives. He knew that they had to deal with their fears, just as you have to deal with yours.

The truth of the matter is that you have to make a decision. Just as Paul warned the church of Corinth, you must decide if you are going to follow God's Word, obey it, and stand with God, or are you going to be motivated by fear? If you allow fear to control you then you will be destroyed.

Fear seems to be a natural part of our lives. We live in a world that's dominated by fear. The television news is depressing. The newspapers are depressing. The murders, the rapes, the wars, planes being blown up, cancer...if you listened to all the reports you couldn't eat anything or drink anything. If you watched all the reports on the wars and the rumors of wars, you'd be biting your finger nails off, wondering if somebody was going to drop the bomb.

The whole world is controlled by fear...fear of dying, fear of war, fear of AIDS. I know people who have an unbelievable fear of AIDS. They don't want to have contact with people or shake the hand of a person they don't know. Their lives are motivated and controlled by fear.

We live in a world that is dominated by fear...fear of death, fear of loneliness, fear of getting old, fear of not having enough money, fear of minorities. There is a new resurgence of prejudice in our country that's spreading from shore to shore. This prejudice is called a fear of mankind. Some white people are saying, "You know, the minorities are getting all the jobs." If you let that fear motivate your life, you will make some very stupid decisions and do some very dumb things. Hatred of minorities is always based on fear.

Fear of losing someone will cause you to act like a fool. It is nothing more than jealousy. The root of jealousy is fear. If you allow jealousy to stay in your life, you will push everyone away from you because of fear.

I wonder how many people would be blessed of God if they weren't so afraid to step out and do what God has called them to do. Fear of failure can keep you in a state of depression. It can keep you isolated, lonely, and even label you as a loser. People who have a fear of failure often never achieve anything in their lives because they are afraid to try. They already believe they will fail. It is God's desire that you live in peace and that you live at rest, free of worry and fear. Worry and fear are of the flesh and it's not for the child of God. We are supposed to walk in the Spirit, and trust God.

I know of people who have a fear of being with others. I received a telephone call from a woman once who hasn't been out of her house in 17 years. She is consumed by uncontrollable fear when she attempts to leave her house.

Then there are those that have a fear of rejection. They are afraid that people will reject them, so they isolate themselves. That is a spirit of fear.

We all have specific fears in our lives. Every one of us has areas in our lives that need to be conquered. Through different circumstances, fears have been introduced into our lives, but through Jesus Christ, you can conquer all of them.

You'll never overcome fear with pills or with a psychiatrist, even though counselors can help you. Your only true help will come through the Word of God and through the Blood of Jesus Christ. How many times have you seen someone so afraid of something that fear eventually overtakes them?

The thing that you fear most will eventually overtake you. However, you can do all things through Christ Jesus who strengthens you, and you are more than a conqueror through Him who loves you. You must remember this, **Greater is He that lives in you than he who lives in the world.**

If you are worried or fearful, then you are not being ruled by the God of peace. It is God's desire for His children to live in peace and not in fear. Romans 14:17 says, **For the kingdom of God is not eating and drinking, but righteousness and peace and joy in the Holy Spirit.** God has peace for you, but it's not the kind of peace that the world understands.

Chapter One

Worry Is Nothing More Than Fear

There are alot of things that we could worry about, however, we must realize that worry is nothing more than fear. To worry means to be anxious, or to be troubled about your future.

"Let not your heart be troubled; believe in God, believe also in Me. In My Father's house are many dwelling places; if it were not so, I would have told you; for I go to prepare a place for you." **John 14:1**

Jesus said, *"Let not your heart be troubled."* Since He's the God of Heaven, what are you so worried about? He is saying, "If I can go to Heaven to prepare a place for you, surely I can take care of your troubles."

The whole 14th chapter of John is written to the church. It's not written to the world. It's written to you and I. Jesus began by saying, *"Don't let your heart be troubled."* In other words, "Chill out, quit worrying and why are you trippin'? I'm going to Heaven and I'm going to take care of you."

God brought the children of Israel out of the land of bondage. He gave them a promise, but they didn't believe it. The children of Israel thought that God wasn't going to take care of them. They felt fear in their hearts and began to question God. They became negative and were absolutely distraught over their future. Their murmuring, back-biting, grumbling, and worrying kept them out of the Promised Land.

Jesus said to quit worrying about your future because He has your future all under control. Worry is nothing more than a form of fear that shows a lack of trust about your future. We know that God does not like it when His people are moved by fear. God is pleased when His people are moved by faith. There are many things we could worry about if we wanted to...our families, jobs, sickness, AIDS, security, the future of this planet, and even our pasts. This world programs us to worry. Fear is something that dominates the entire world, and uncertainty is everywhere.

Worry vs. Faith

Every 18 minutes someone in this country dies from stomach cancer or stomach ulcers. The doctors believe the majority of it is brought on by worry. The Bible says in Romans 14:23 that *...whatever is not from faith is sin.* Worry is sin. Worry is a thief. Most of what you worry about never comes to pass. You cannot change anything by worrying. The only thing worry will do is make you so depressed no one will want to be around you.

But My righteous one shall live by faith; And if he shrinks back, my soul has no pleasure in him.
Hebrews 10:38

You must believe God is working things out and you must refuse to worry. Faith says, "I trust You, Lord." Worry says, "Oh, my God, my world's falling apart." Worry, like fear, is the opposite of faith. The Christian walk is learning how to trust the Lord in spite of circumstances. Growing up in Christ is learning how to walk by faith, not by sight.

You must learn to cast all your fears on Him. "Lord, I cast all my fears on you. I cast all my cares on you, for I know you care for me." Don't live a life of fear. Live a life of faith.

Are you going to put your faith into action and follow the Word of God and not let your heart be troubled? Jesus said, *"Peace I leave with you."* If you are born-again, there is peace available to you that the world cannot comprehend or understand. Jesus wants you to take His peace and not worry about your future because He has it all under control.

Paul said in Philippians 3 to put your past behind you and to press ahead. Even if you have a terrible past, commit it to God, sell out to Him, and serve God with all your heart. Let the Blood of Jesus wash your past away.

Casting all your anxiety upon Him, because He cares for you. **I Peter 5:7**

Cast your worries on Him because He cares for you. It's time that you learn how to cast those burdens on the Lord. It's time you let the great burden-bearer carry your burdens. Jesus is your burden-bearer. You are not equipped to carry your burdens, but Jesus is equipped to carry them for you.

Refuse to worry! If you are staying awake at night worrying about your problems, then you are not casting your cares on Him. God loves you and wants you to quit worrying about your future and start trusting in Him and learn that He will get you through every trial and every tribulation. You <u>can</u> change. You don't have to continue to be fearful and worry the rest of your life. Even if you come from a family of worriers, there is no excuse for a Bible-believing, Blood-bought believer in Jesus Christ to live in doubt, unbelief, and worry.

Jesus Brings The Victory

But thanks be to God, who always leads us in His

triumph in Christ, and manifests through us the sweet aroma of the knowledge of Him in every place.
II Corinthians 2:14

You cannot be defeated. The word "triumph" in Greek means, like a Roman general who has conquered a particular province or a particular enemy. When that general would come home victorious, the senate would reward the conquering general by giving him a parade through the streets of Rome. The general would be clad in purple linen, jewels, gold, ivory, and would be drawn by a team of white horses. Preceding his chariot would be musicians leading the processional singing and giving praises to the general, while others would string flowers everywhere to give honor to that general.

That's what Jesus has done for us. He has already conquored your enemy. *Thanks be to God who always leads us in His triumph in Christ.* You belong to God and the same victory that belongs to Jesus belongs to you. You will always triumph through Christ.

Our God loves us and He's not mad at us. The Word tells us that God will even take what the enemy means to destroy us with and turn it for our good. It is amazing that we serve a God who is so big and so magnificent that He can even take what is meant to harm us, and turn it for our good. In fact, the Word of God says that He'll always cause us to triumph in Christ. ALWAYS means ALWAYS!

A woman recently told me a story about her son. She told me that he had grown up in a Christian home, but was not living for the Lord, and was in fact, living with his girlfriend. Her son and his girlfriend had some domestic problems and he ended up in jail. The mother went on to say, "Pastor, my son is in jail and his life is a mess. However, he gave his life to the Lord Jesus again and now he has hope, peace, and the promise of a new life through Christ Jesus. Sure enough, He brought us from tribulation to triumph."

If you are living right and doing right, no weapon formed against you shall prosper. Weapons will come, but they will not accomplish what they were sent to do. Your God has it all under control and He will always bring you to victory. He will always take you to victory as long as you stand with Him and continue to serve Him. When God brings the victory, all those around you are going to know of God's goodness and that sweet aroma of victory which will surround you.

God Will Turn It For Your Good

And we know that God causes all things to work together for good to those who love God, to those who are called according to His purpose. **Romans 8:28**

If you love God, if you are serving God, if you are living right and are doing right, then you can rest assured that God will turn things for your good. Every cloud has a silver lining. People who display negative attitudes are people who usually look at their circumstances and see only the negative side. People with positive attitudes look for the silver lining inside the cloud!

Not everything that happens to you is God's will. We all experience fires in our lives. Most of the time, we bring the fires upon ourselves. Why do fires come? Fires come to burn out impurities. Trust God in the middle of the fire, even if you don't understand it. He is the potter and you are the clay. He loves you and won't let you stay in the mess that you are in. He loves you enough to turn up the heat sometimes, but it will all work to your good.

The question is this: Are you living right? If you aren't obedient to the Word, you've got some real reasons to start worrying. If you aren't obedient to the Word, God's hand of protection may be off of you. Sell out to God, obey the Word, and He will turn everything for your good.

Therefore, my beloved brethren whom I long to see, my joy and crown, so stand firm in the Lord, my beloved.
Philippians 4:1

God is patient with us because He sees what we are going to be, not what we are. When we came to God, we were a mess, but now He's perfecting us and molding us into His image. Stand firm in the Lord. When you have compromise in your life and you are not following the Word of God, you will be weak and will ask yourself why life isn't working for you. Depression and loneliness can overtake you. The only way to have peace in your life is to sell out to God.

Be anxious for nothing, but in everything by prayer and supplication with thanksgiving let your requests be made known to God. **Philippians 4:6**

You'll never make it without prayer. The only way you can cast your cares upon the Lord is if you are in prayer. Webster defines supplication "to ask for humbly or earnestly through prayer." So, go ahead and cry your heart out to God! Remember, the key here is prayer and supplication with thanksgiving.

The children of Israel were grumbling and negative. "I can't believe this is happening to me, the more I try, the worse it gets."

Don't be like the children of Israel. Instead, thank Him for being a good God...thank Him for having it all under control...thank Him for causing you to triumph always in Christ. Praise Him in all things!

And the peace of God, which surpasses all comprehension, shall guard your hearts and your minds in Christ Jesus. **Philippians 4:7**

God promises us in verse 7 that He will guard our hearts and minds with His peace, and that the peace we receive from Him will be different. It will be beyond what we can understand. Everyone wants peace in their lives. World governments make war in the name of peace. People search for peace in drugs, alcohol, and sex. However, God tells us in His Word that we will only have peace when we cast our cares and burdens upon Him.

God Is In Charge

"For this reason I say to you do not be anxious for your life, as to what you shall eat, or what you shall drink; nor for your body, as to what you shall put on. Is not life more than food, and the body than clothing? Look at the birds of the air, that they do not sow, neither do they reap, nor gather into barns, and yet your heavenly Father feeds them. Are you not worth much more than they?" **Matthew 6:25**

If God can take care of the birds, He can take care of you. Isn't God ultimately in charge of your life? Situations may not ever work out the way you think they should, but they are going to work out one way or another. Even when all looks lost, it's not over yet. When they crucified Jesus on the cross, it was Friday.

All looked lost. But Sunday was coming. Your Sunday is coming as well. Don't worry. Our God has it all under control.

> *Finally, brethren, whatever is true, whatever is honorable, whatever is right, whatever is pure, whatever is lovely, whatever is of good repute, if there is any excellence and if anything worthy of praise, let your mind dwell on these things.* **Philippians 4:8**

Sometimes your mind tells you things are bad. However, things are never as bad as your mind tells you they are. Think of the Lord! Think of God! Think of pure things! Don't let your mind go off on tangents. When your mind begins to wander, just begin to speak the Word of God out of your mouth.

Your mind may say things like "My child is on drugs and he's going to hell!" You must speak God's Word out of your mouth. For example in Acts 16:31, God's Word says, **"You and your household shall be saved."** When your mind gets to talking trash, you must say what God's Word says. Say, "Thank You Jesus that according to Your Word in Acts 16:31, my child is saved, he's going to Heaven, and there's no weapon that is formed against him that shall prosper. Lord, I turn this entire situation over to You, and I praise You that Your Word is true."

God expects you to pray with thanksgiving and to praise Him in all situations, and to grow up in Christ and do what the Word of God tells you to do. It's a decision that you have to make. You can either get mad at God, or you can cast your cares upon Him. You have a choice.

You may be going through a difficult time in your life right now, and question why God isn't answering your prayers. Spiritual maturity is the perseverance to stand knowing that your answer is going to be manifested. There are some things you are never going to figure out, especially when you are in the middle of it. But when you are through it, you can look back and see how God protected you. *If God be for you, who can be against you!*

Difficulties come to everybody, but my God is going to take care of them. You are the sheep of His pasture. He is the shepherd. You have been bought with a price, and now you belong to Him. He's going to take care of you.

Chapter Two

Peace in the Middle of the Storm

No matter how much money you have, you cannot buy peace. You can buy things, you can buy vacations, you can buy drugs, you can buy the best doctors, but you cannot buy peace. Jesus came to bring peace to His people. There is a war going on in the spiritual realm that you cannot see with your natural eye. The spiritual forces of darkness try to align themselves against your household in such a way as to kill, steal, and destroy. If you aren't aware of this spiritual war being fought over your life, you can't possibly understand the importance of having Jesus Christ as your Savior. You need Jesus in your life to show you how to be victorious and how to be more than a conqueror. I want you to know that Jesus will bring you peace in the middle of every storm.

Walk In Faith

You have no doubt heard the expression, "Keep the faith, baby." In the middle of every storm that comes into our lives, we have a choice as to how we react to that particular storm. We can either keep our eyes on Jesus and walk in faith, or we can look at the circumstances that surround our situation. Peter needed to make that same choice in Matthew 14:28-31:

> *And Peter answered Him and said, "Lord, if it is You, command me to come to you on the water." And He said, "Come!" And Peter got out of the boat, and walked on the water and came toward Jesus. But seeing the wind, he became afraid, and beginning to sink, he cried out, saying "Lord, save me!" And immediately Jesus stretched out His hand and took hold of him, and said to him, "O*

you of little faith, why did you doubt?"

Peter said, "If that's you walking out there on the water, just tell me and I'll get out of the boat and walk with you. If you command me to do something, I can do it." Jesus said, "Come on, Peter, come on." And Peter got out of the boat and began to walk on the water. You can imagine the faith that rises up in your heart when you see a miracle taking place in your own life. Peter's miracle was happening, but then he took his eyes off Jesus. He began to look at the wind and at the waves blowing up against his ankles, and he said, "Whoa, wait a minute...this is an impossibility, I can't do this." Then Peter began to sink. He cried out to the Lord and the Lord saved him and got him back into the boat. Jesus said to him, *"Oh you of little faith, why did you doubt?"* (Vs 31) In other words, "Why aren't you single minded? Why are you double minded? Why are you wavering in your faith? If I tell you to do something, don't you know that I am there with you, I will never leave you or forsake you? I am there until the end of time. If I called you to do something, I'll equip you to do it."

Don't Let Fear Stop Your Miracle

Before you actually see your miracle, fear may come in and try to overtake you and stop the miracle in your life. The main tool that the enemy uses to control our lives is fear. Fear is an anxiety that expects danger. God is moved by faith. Jesus said that your spiritual enemy is the devil. The devil uses fear to control you and to guide your life. Fear will always come in if you take your eyes off Jesus. That's why it's so important to be in the Word every single day.

Peter started out in faith, but fear stopped his miracle. If you allow fear in your life, you will never step out in faith. You'll never do what God's called you to do. There are many that God has called to do something for Him, but because of fear in their lives they are afraid to get out of the boat and do it.

Fear and faith are diabolically opposed. Faith trusts and believes, but fear is full of doubt and unbelief. If you make certain decisions in your life while being motivated by fear, you will make a wrong decision every single time. However, if you make up your mind to obey the Word, even though fear would come against your mind, you will always be victorious because God and His Word are one. God's Word is mighty and powerful and sharper than any two-edged sword.

Perhaps you need a miracle in your finances. If you listen to what your mind tells you, you'll never give financially to God. You'll sit there and say, "When God makes me prosperous or rich, I'll give to Him." Fear holds you back. The fear of not having enough money is the thing that's keeping you from giving to God. Not giving to God is the very thing that's keeping the financial miracles from happening in your life. You have to make up your mind to obey and follow the Word, even if you don't understand it, even if it's against what you feel. You cannot allow fear to dominate your life. You will never become what God wants you to be, and you will never make the decisions God wants you to make, as long as fear controls you.

The Christian walk is a walk that teaches us to overcome prejudice, fear, and the things that keep us bound to our past. If you are dealing with one or more of these areas in your life, you need to get close to Jesus Christ because Jesus is your answer. I'm not talking about religion, or how many times you come to church. I'm talking about a personal relationship between you and the risen Savior, Jesus Christ.

Jesus Will Bring You Peace

These things I have spoken to you, that in Me you may have peace. In the world you have tribulation, but take courage, I have overcome the world. **John 16:33**

Religion will never bring you peace. People and things will never bring you peace. Only Jesus can bring you peace. His Word says that He has overcome the world. He's not only overcome your problem, He has overcome the world.

We still read the Old Testament because it's the Word of God. In the Old Covenant the Sabbath day was a 24 hour period of time where the people entered into complete rest. Jesus is the fulfillment in the New Covenant of the Sabbath day. In Him you have complete rest, not only one day a week, but seven days a week. Being a disciple of Jesus Christ doesn't stop the storms in life. You will never escape the difficulties and problems of life. Adversity comes upon every one of us, but if you love Jesus, you can have peace in the middle of every storm.

We must all take courage, stop worrying, and chill out. That's my translation of John 16:33. *If God be for you, who can be against you?* You can face every adversity and still have peace in the middle of the storm. Don't ask me how this works, I don't know. All I know is that I can be in the middle of the biggest storm I've ever seen in my life, go to God, draw close to Him, and He gives me the peace that surpasses all understanding. I can't explain it. I can only tell you that there is peace in the middle of the storm, because He is the Prince of Peace.

Jesus said to the religious leaders, *"Come to me all ye who are weary and heavy-laden and I will give you rest."* He was saying, "Man, you aren't going to have any rest in religion, but you will have rest in Me. You'll never have peace in religion. You'll only have peace through Me." We live in the days where times are difficult. Crime is at its worst and destruction is everywhere. But you can't allow fear to control you. What is your response in the middle of the storm? Are you afraid to go out at night? What fears are holding you back? What fears are keeping you from becoming what God has called you to be?

Blessed is the man who trusts in the Lord And whose trust is the Lord. For he will be like a tree planted by the water, That extends its roots by a stream And will not fear when the heat comes; But it's leaves will be green, And it will not be anxious in a year of drought Nor cease to yield fruit. **Jeremiah 17:7-8**

Extend Your Roots

It's not an easy thing to learn to trust God. It's a life long process. It's a process every day, every month, and every year of learning to give a little more of your life to God, and learning how you can trust Him a little more as you walk with Him. He says if you will trust in Him, you'll be like a tree that is planted by the water and extends its roots by the stream...you will not fear when the difficulties of life come your way.

In this world you shall have tribulation, but Jesus said, "Do not worry about it, don't sweat it, for I have overcome the world." Jesus said, "Chill-out, I have it all under control." If your trust is in the Lord, your roots will extend down to the deep places, way below the ground. When the heat comes, when the pressure comes, when the difficulties come, you'll not wilt, you'll stay green, you'll still produce fruit, and you won't be shaken by the difficulties of life.

In other words, no matter what the economy does, you're still going to be blessed if you are serving God and trusting in Him. No matter how the difficulties of life may come against you, no matter what your friends do...all may even abandon you...but, if you're planted by that stream and trusting in Him, you're going to yield good fruit continually in your life.

"Peace I leave with you; My peace I give to you; not as the world gives, do I give to you. Let not your heart be troubled, nor let it be fearful." **John 14:27**

Jesus is telling you, "I give you peace." It's not the kind of peace that the world promises. He said, "Don't let your heart be troubled or be afraid. When you have a decision to make, are you going to trust Me in the middle of the storm, or not?" You see, this world is a place of much fear and trembling. There is a place where you can find safety. There is place where you can find security from all harm. It's in the arms of our loving Lord and Savior, Jesus Christ.

I remember seeing a painting depicting a raging storm. The waves were crashing against a rock wall. It was raining, lightening was flashing, and in the cleft of a rock there was a little bird just whistling and singing without a care in the world. The Lord showed me that the life of a born-again believer in Jesus Christ is much the same way. The world can quake around us, and times can be difficult, but we can have a song in the middle of the storm. We can have peace in the middle of the storm because we know in Whom we trust.

Difficulties Will Arise

We all know that we live in troubled times. Jesus said, "Don't sweat it. Don't be worried. Cast all your cares on Me." Don't let fear rule your life. Don't you know Jesus said, "I'm on board your ship"? You can overcome fear if Jesus is on board your ship of life.

It's so sad to see Christians operating in fear and worry. We're not ruled by the economy of this world. We're ruled by the Word of God and the Blood of Jesus Christ. I don't care if they drop the bomb and if all the warehouses are out of food. If God has to send the ravens to feed me, He will, because He's the God that promised to meet all of my needs according to His riches in glory by Christ Jesus. Jesus said, *"Peace I leave with you and peace I give to you."* Do you have peace today? Jesus said, *"Let not your heart be troubled, nor let it be fearful."* As long as God is on His throne, you have no reason to panic.

You can face every trial, every difficulty, and every hardship. You can do it with peace because the Prince of Peace lives within your heart. He came to bring you the gospel of peace. *Greater is He that lives in me than he that lives in the world.* Ephesians 6:15 says, *having shod your feet with the preparation of the gospel of peace.* It's a decision you have to make everyday. Are you going to walk in peace or are you going to walk in fear? Don't go around saying, "Oh, I can't believe this is happening to me," or "I'm afraid of this, I'm afraid of that." The Word of God says, *"My God has not given me a spirit of fear but of power, love, and a sound mind."* You are going to have to make a decision to line up with the Word of God, to say what God's Word says, and not to panic when you see things going wrong around you.

Jesus was talking to the man who had the epileptic son. Demons threw the little boy on the ground and he began to foam at the mouth and roll in the fire. Jesus didn't panic and say, "Oh my God, get him up here, get him up here." He said, "How long has your boy been like this?" Don't panic when you see the difficult times around you. Trust in Him. If there is something that has gone wrong in your life, you don't need to panic, God is still on His throne.

Joseph could have panicked, but he didn't. He was in prison for years. Joseph was faithful right where he was. He didn't question God. God used him in such a way that he became the keeper of the prison. No matter where you are, if you stay faithful to God, He'll use you in a great and powerful way.

If you are living right and doing right, you have nothing to fear in your life. If you aren't living right and if you aren't doing right, then you have a lot to worry about, and you have a lot to be fearful over. Get right with God and you can eliminate the fear in your life.

To grant us that we, being delivered from the hand of our enemies, Might serve Him without fear. **Luke 1:74**

Luke 1:74 says that when the Messiah comes, He'll deliver you from the hand of the enemy and then you can serve God without fear. I want you to know that Jesus is the Messiah and He's already come. Draw close to Him through the Word of God. Jesus has already defeated your spiritual enemy. Victory is already yours. Remember what Jesus said: *"Peace I leave with you and My peace I give to you not as the world gives."*

How The World Finds Peace

The world's way of getting peace is through pills, meditation, blanking your mind to nothingness, or chanting for peace. The new movement in the world is to look within yourself to find peace. If you look inside yourself and Jesus isn't there, the only thing you're going to find is an empty vacuum. You can kid yourself all you want, but there is nothing inside you that will lift you out of depression and fear except the Lord. Everything else is just an illusion.

The world says surrender your mind to nothingness. That only leaves you empty. Jesus said He will fill you with peace, not with emptiness.

This book of the law shall not depart from your mouth, but you shall meditate on it day and night, so that you may be careful to do according to all that is written in it; for then you will make your way prosperous, and then you will have success. **Joshua 1:8**

In other words, it says to get the Word of God down inside you. Speak the Word out of your mouth and meditate on it day and night. Obey the Word of God and you will have success in your life. If you want to know how to have success, just follow the Word of God.

Demons seek empty minds. You need to fill your mind with the knowledge of the Word of God. It's the Word that will set you free. There are many activities that can open up your mind to the demonic realm...drugs, alcohol, pornography, witchcraft, and horoscopes. One thing is absolutely certain, you will never be victorious as long as you are playing church and dabbling in sin.

The Peace of God

Be anxious for nothing, but in everything by prayer and supplication with thanksgiving let your requests be made known to God. And the peace of God, which surpasses all comprehension, shall guard your hearts

and your minds in Christ Jesus. Finally, brethren, whatever is true, whatever is honorable, whatever is right, whatever is pure, whatever is lovely, whatever is of good repute, if there is any excellence and if anything worthy of praise, let your mind dwell on these things.
Philippians 4:6-8

If you'll pray with thanksgiving THEN the peace of God that passes all understanding shall guard your heart and your MIND in Christ Jesus. You must dwell on the things of God. When your mind goes off on a tangent and starts to dwell on "Oh my God, I've got cancer," start dwelling on the Word of God. The Word of God says, **By His stripes I am healed**. The Word of God says, **He sent the Word and healed them**. You must make a decision to dwell on the Word of God. Most of the time it's nothing more than an imagination in your mind anyway.

The steadfast of mind Thou wilt keep in perfect peace. Because he trusts in Thee. **Isaiah 26:3**

If your mind is steadfast on the Lord Jesus Christ you will be in perfect peace. If fear is dominating your life, you need to get as close to Jesus as you possibly can. You see, fear cannot stay in the presence of our Lord.

Perfect Love Casts Out Fear

There is no fear in love; but perfect love casts out fear, because fear involves punishment, and the one who fears is not perfected in love. **I John 4:18**

Think about this scripture for just a minute: *Perfect love casts out fear*. That means if you do something to me, instead of me reacting to you, I operate in love. Sometimes I may not want to. My mind may be saying, "Just bust them in the chops, and then repent later." However, you can't listen to your mind. You must operate in love. If you operated in love in every situation you wouldn't have fear in your life. Fear will keep you from becoming what God wants you to be. Love never fails.

What about love? When you truly know that God loves you, then you can enter into every difficulty in life without fear, knowing that He has it all under control. He <u>cannot</u> fail. Let Him fight the battles. You must remember, perfect love casts out fear. God loves you and has your best interests at heart. Because of His love, you don't have to let fear work in your life. In other words, when the bottom falls out of your life, don't panic. Say, "My God is working it out. My God is working a plan for me."

It is extremely important to remember to speak God's Word over specific fears in your life. When you say things like, "Perfect love casts out fear," or "many are the afflictions (or the troubles, or the difficulties) of the righteous, but the Lord delivers him out of them *ALL*," faith will overtake you, and soon you will begin to feel the peace and joy of God in your life.

We all go through storms in our lives. None of us are exempt from the storms of life. You cannot look at the storm when it arises. The human reaction is to focus on the storm, on the problem, on the difficulties, until fear comes into your life, and then you are controlled by that fear. You cannot look at the storm. You must look to the Lord Jesus Christ....He is love.

Fear can't control you if you know how much God loves you. God loves you so much that He will take what the enemy means to destroy you with, and He will turn it for your good.

Chapter Three
Be Careful What You Say

My God has not given me a spirit of fear, but of power and love and a sound mind. **II Timothy 1:7**

God has given you three resources to overcome fear. These three resources are His power, His love, and a sound and disciplined mind. When fears come against your mind, don't talk about them. The more you talk about them the more they'll grow and the bigger they'll get. Don't talk about how big your mountains are. Tell your mountains how big your God is.

Just before I went on a mission's trip to the Soviet Union, someone came to me and said, "Pastor, as I prayed, God showed me that all hell is mounting an attack against you. When you go into the Soviet Union all of hell is going to come against you." Tell me something new!

You can always tell if someone is motivated by fear or if they are motivated by faith. What are they talking about? What are they speaking out of their mouths? Be careful what you say because your faith will never grow greater than what you are saying. That's why your confession must line up with the Word of God. I'm talking about standing on the Word of God and living for God. No matter who you are, you must face every fear or it will eventually destroy you. Fear is not going to go away. You must deal with it.

Sometimes fear overcomes me and I have to fake it. I just have to say, "My God has not given me a spirit of fear, but power, and love and a sound mind." A few years ago I decided I was going to ride a motorcycle and I wasn't going to be afraid anymore. When I get on the motorcycle and start riding, I begin to say, "My God has not given me a spirit of fear, but power and love and a sound mind." You have to face your fears. If you run from your fears, they will overtake you and eat you up, and you will be in a prison for the rest of your life. Remember this, *"Greater is He that lives in me than he that lives in the world."* Also remember, *"My God has not given me a spirit of fear."*

Death and life are in the power of the tongue. And those who love it will eat its fruit. **Proverbs 18:21**

You'll eat the fruit of the things you are saying with your mouth. If you are talking worry and fear, you are going to eat the fruit of that. If you are talking faith, you are going to eat the fruit of that, eventually. Start changing your words. Negative words will affect your attitude and affect your faith. When worry comes against your mind, grow up in Christ and cast your worries on Him and don't say the negative things you want to say. Your words can increase your faith or destroy your faith. Trust God no matter what you see. Refuse to worry. Leave no room in your life for fear.

Fear, many times, comes into our lives just by the words that we say. "I'm afraid to die." "I'm afraid of being alone." "I'm afraid of cancer." So many times we invite fear into our lives by the words that we say. The Bible plainly tells us that we will have what we say, eventually. I'm not talking about name it and claim it, or gab it and grab it, and all that business. If you're saying what the Word of God says, you will eventually have what the Word of God says.

If you are speaking fear out of your mouth, then according to Proverbs 6:2, *you will be snared with the words of your mouth*. Job said, "The thing I feared most came upon me." Think about that statement. You'll talk about the thing you fear the most until it comes to pass. You'll say it, and say it, and say it, until you've got it. What are you saying about your marriage? What are you saying about your job? What are you saying about your Pastor? Understand the importance of speaking only that which is in agreement with God's Word.

Now let me tell you a little secret. Say what God says. That is what faith is all about. You stand, you stand, you stand, and you stand! After you've done all, you stand. How long do you stand? I don't know. After you've done all you know to do, you stand. The flesh says, "Don't you do that." The flesh says, "Bail out now." The flesh wants to quit. It doesn't want to fight. But the Word of God says, *If God be for me who can be against me?*

Your mind is a great battlefield. Most of what you worry about never happens and worry always distorts the truth tremendously. Don't entertain those negative thoughts. You can't help it if negative thoughts come into your mind, but you don't have to let them stay there. You cannot let those negative thoughts dominate your thinking.

Don't give life to your worries and fears by talking about them all the time. Change your words. Say, "My God is taking care of me." Start confessing your faith in the living God instead of your pessimistic thoughts that continually dominate your mind.

It's only a matter of time until you will triumph. God will take you to victory and cause every bad thing to be turned for your good. He's the King of Glory! He's the King of Heaven! He's already defeated your spiritual enemy. Therefore, refuse to walk in fear. Change your words, change your attitude, and choose to walk in faith.

God Tests The Heart

I the Lord, search the heart, I test the mind. Even to give to each man according to his ways, According to the results of his deeds. **Jeremiah 17:10**

Life is going to test your stand of faith. God is going to find out whether you have faith in your heart or not. How do you react when trials come into your life? Do you say "Oh God, I'm destroyed, I can't believe this is happening to me," or do you stand in faith? Commit your situation to the Lord and don't let anything steal your faith. One day, out of nowhere, when you least expect it, your answer will come.

One of the primary reasons Christians are defeated is they give in to fears that come against them. Fears will come against every single one of us. However, I'm not moved by what I see. I'm only moved by what God's Word says. I will be tested. I either give in to the fear, or I stand in faith.

If you allow fear to stay in your life, you will never do anything for God to any extent. There will always be some reason why you can't do something for God. You don't have enough money. You don't have enough education. You don't have the right skin color. You're too tall or too short. The main reason people aren't bold witnesses for Jesus Christ is because they're afraid of what somebody might think of them. They're afraid of being rejected.

Stand In Faith

People who have nervous breakdowns or nervous conditions are people who are controlled by a spirit of fear. Many doctor bills are a result of a spirit of fear. "I'm afraid I've got something wrong with me." So, you go to the doctor. They do test after test, only to find out there's nothing wrong with you.

We are to stand up in the face of every storm and say, "No, you will not have me." We're to stand up in the face of every storm and say, "I'm not afraid of you." Fear should not be in the life of an overcoming Christian. You grew up with weak areas in your life. You must recognize them, face them for what they are and say, "I will not live like this any more." You're going to have to make that choice and that decision. If you're a born-again believer in Jesus Christ, fear has no right in your life. You can face every battle in your life knowing that the King of Heaven has already defeated the king of hell.

The Fight Of Faith

And without faith it is impossible to please Him, for he who comes to God must believe that He is, and that He is a rewarder of those who seek Him. **Hebrews 11:6**

It's very easy to walk by what you see rather than what the Word of God says. In fact, it's natural to go by sight rather than by faith. The Bible tells us that God is motivated by faith. It's very important that you understand that our spiritual enemy, the devil, motivates by fear. There are natural fears in our lives and some are good, but if that fear is uncontrolled, it can be bad. The enemy desires fear to come to such a point in our lives that it controls us and we no longer make decisions based on truth. Instead, we make decisions based on fear.

As long as fear is controlling your life, you will never operate in faith. How can you please God? How can you exhibit faith in God if you allow fear to stay? You can't! If fear is operating in your life, faith cannot operate. You see, the devil's kingdom is perpetuated through fear. That's the way he does everything. The only way the enemy can truly control you is if you allow fear to stay.

Paul told Timothy to fight the good fight of faith. The *fight* is **FAITH**. The fight is **NOT** the devil. He has already been defeated. The fight is **MY** *faith*, and I proclaim the enemy is defeated by the Blood of the Lamb and I testify of his defeat. He's already been rendered powerless. God has a great plan for you, but if the enemy can get you to move in fear he can stop God's plan. You must trust the Lord. You can't go by what you see and you can't go by what you feel.

The enemy cannot defeat you if you know who you are in Jesus Christ. You need to look at it this way, the devil is firing his shots, but they're blanks. They are lies. If you don't believe his lies, you'll make it. If he throws fear at you, have faith. On the surface faith looks absolutely too difficult. On the surface it looks impossible, as if it's something you cannot do. II Corinthians 10:3-5 says:

For though we walk in the flesh, we do not war according to the flesh, for the weapons of our warfare are not of the flesh, but divinely powerful for the destruction of fortresses. We are destroying speculations and every lofty thing raised up against the knowledge of God, and we are taking every thought captive to the obedience of Christ.

In other words, it is a spiritual fight. Our fight is the fight of faith in the spiritual realm. It's a decision that we make. Stand in faith or run in fear. Our weapons are not knives, guns, or tanks. Our weapons are in the spiritual realm against the enemy. The thoughts that come against our minds that are contrary to the Word of God must be taken captive. *As a man thinketh, so is he*. If you dwell on it, if you think on it, you will become that which you think on, whether it be good or bad. You must be determined to overcome every fear that tries to dominate your life.

Chapter Four

Fear Of The Future

People today are desperately afraid of their futures. They are afraid of what the future holds for their families. Why do people go to fortune tellers to have tarot cards and their palms read? They seek after signs and wonders, and after people who can tell them what their future holds, because they have a tremendous fear of the future. There are no crystal balls that you can gaze into that will show you what road to take, or house to buy, or if a particular job is "the right one." God alone holds your future in the palm of His hand, and His Word can tell you the future.

Now it shall be, if you will diligently obey the Lord your God being careful to do all His commandments which I command you today, the Lord your God will set you high above all the nations of the earth. And all these blessings shall come upon you and overtake you if you will obey the Lord your God. **Deuteronomy 28:1-2**

Many times you can see what the future holds for people by the fruit in their life, and how they live their life in accordance with God's Word. Deuteronomy 28 says, *Serve God and He will command blessings on you.* If you don't serve Him then curses will overtake you. Your future directly parallels the way you serve the Lord. If you serve Him with all your heart and soul, and you're living right and doing right, blessings will overtake you. You will be blessed coming in and going out. However, if you don't have a relationship with the Lord, and you live your life to gratify your flesh, you will have a miserable existence. Your future will hold nothing but fear and misery.

We have a spiritual enemy who plans strategies against us. One of those strategies is to introduce fear into our lives so he can dominate and control us for the rest of our life. His desire is to find our weaknesses.

Every person has a weak area in their life. You might have it hidden from other people, but I guarantee you, your spiritual enemy knows your weaknesses. He doesn't come at you in your strengths, but in your weaknesses, whether it's sex or drugs or maybe some specific fears in your life.

We are all born with natural fears. Natural fears are good because they nurture self preservation.

The enemy's strategy is to dominate you in a particular area, and make you a prisoner of your fears. His plan is to make you feel so afraid that you're unable to overcome a specific fear in your life. That fear actually holds you captive.

I met someone not very long ago who wouldn't come to church at night. This person had so much fear he was actually afraid to leave his house after the sun went down. We all have specific fears in our lives that are usually caused by a certain incident in our past. You see, your mind is like a computer. It compiles all of the data around you, and says, "Be careful, look out, you're going to get it, be afraid." It's a natural defense mechanism.

How Fear Enters Our Lives

Fear enters our lives in several ways. Let me give you an example of specific fears that are introduced into our lives. When a parent loses a child, they can develop an unnatural fear of losing other children. If they are not careful, it will become an obsession. When it becomes an obsession, it becomes a dominating force that controls their lives. You see, the devil is a thief who comes to steal, kill, and destroy. As the enemy magnifies that fear in your life, he has actually put in motion a strategy, to steal your happiness. I know of a couple that had such a fear of not being able to get pregnant, that the woman couldn't conceive. They eventually started adoption proceedings, and within three months the wife became pregnant. The power of fear is absolutely incredible.

When a person has a bad sexual experience, like being raped, it can develop into an unnatural fear. If it goes unchecked, it will dominate and control that person for the rest of their life. They will be afraid to date. Fear can become so prevalent in their lives they may be afraid to leave their homes.

When I was a child, my father was a painting contractor and I used to go with him to the out-of-town sites. On one of those contracting jobs, he was painting a Post Office. I remember my dad being up on a scaffold and minutes later I was climbing up the scaffold after him. I didn't think anything about it. But the scaffold moved and a fear was introduced into my life at that point. From that day forward I was afraid of heights.

The enemy will use those natural fears and try to magnify them, holding us in bondage. If you allow the fear of heights to go unchecked, you may not be able to go into a tall building. Maybe you need to conduct business there, but you cannot because you're afraid.

I know people that are desperately afraid of flying. Flying is one of the safest ways in the world to travel. It's safer than traveling by car or train.

If someone locked you in a dark room when you where a child, you are probably afraid of the dark, or at least afraid of being left alone. The enemy will try to use that to dominate and control you, and put you in bondage.

If your earthly father was harsh and cruel, then you are probably afraid of God. You probably have a very difficult time trusting and believing in your Heavenly Father.

If you were raised by a dominating parent that controlled you, one that didn't lead you but controlled your life, you probably have a strong fear of being controlled today. Anytime you get around someone that has a strong personality, something rises up inside you. It's a fear that someone is going to dominate you and make you do something you don't want to do.

There are people today that have great problems with authority, whether it's a pastor, or a policeman, or any kind of authority figure. Somewhere in their life they were dominated to the point that they hate authority because someone was cruel to them in their past. And of course, when someone grows up with an unhealthy, unnatural fear of being controlled, you can imagine the problems that occur in their marriage. You can't even raise your voice, in any way, without short circuiting their brain.

Fear is a tool that the enemy uses to control our lives. In order to please God we must exhibit faith in Him. Faith and fear are opposites, just like the North Pole and the South Pole. If you allow fear to dominate you, God's plan will be stopped in your life. Let me say it again. God's plan cannot be manifest in your life, if you allow fear to control you.

That's what prejudice is all about. It's one race that is afraid of another race. They are afraid of things that happened in the past and afraid of differences. We want people to be like us. When someone is different, in some way, we're afraid of that difference. Fear of whites. Fear of blacks. Fear of whatever. Fear causes people to hate. When we think that someone is getting an advantage over us, we often become fearful. If you're not careful, hate will begin to control your life.

It's like affirmative action. Affirmative action is an action that's trying to make better the injustices of the past. If you're not careful, you will look at affirmative action and say that these guys are trying to get my job, rather than seeing it for what it is, an attempt to make up for the injustices of the past. You need to trust God. God, not man, is supposed to be your source.

The Word of God is the Only Answer

The enemy will try to dominate you and control your emotions and your feelings with fear. Once fear becomes our motivation, once you feel threatened, it's very difficult to trust God the way you should. The Word of God is the only answer. It doesn't make any difference what color you are. The Word of God is your answer. The government is not your answer. The government has proven they can't solve your problems. When difficulties come, begin to say, "If God be for me who can stand against me?" God's Word works for everybody the same way.

You have to start getting the Word of God down on the inside of you. You have to follow the principals in the Word of God. Speak the Word of God, stand on the Word of God, and live in the Word of God. What He has done for me, He will do for you. What He did for Moses, He will do for you. When fear is your motivation, you will make wrong decisions every single time. Have you ever made a decision in a certain situation while you were walking in fear? Ninety-nine times out of a hundred, you'll make the wrong decision. You'll think at the time you are making the right decision. You do the dumbest things when you're operating in fear, because fear is the opposite of faith. Whatever decision you're trying to make, whatever you think you should do in a fearful situation, do the opposite, and it will probably be the correct one.

The bottom line is fear. An example is tithing to God. "I'm afraid if I give to God I won't have enough to pay my bills, and then I'll have bad credit." The enemy controls through fear.

You know the story about the unfaithful steward. To one He gave one talent, to another He gave two talents, and to another He gave five talents. The man with five talents took them and went and did something with them, and he received five additional talents. The man with two talents went out and worked. He worked hard and he received two additional talents. But the one that received one talent was so afraid of losing it, that he hid it. So Jesus said, "Give me that talent. I'm going to take it away from you and give it to this guy over here." You see, fear was that man's motivation. Fear controlled him and caused him to be unfaithful. If fear is operating in your life, it will cause you to be unfaithful to God. The enemy tries to get you to operate in fear, so he can control you, direct your life, and ultimately stop God's plan for your life.

Fear will always cause you to make the wrong decision. One of the enemy's greatest ways to keep people out of the ministry is the use of fear... fear to step out in faith, fear that God won't meet your needs, fear that you will look like a fool. Oh God, I can't go pray for that man, what if he doesn't get healed? Fear of being broke, fear of not having enough will paralyze you. Fears will control you and keep you from being faithful to God.

Chapter Five

How To Overcome Specific Fears

Number One: Repent of your sins. Sin is an open doorway for the enemy. When you operate in fear that will open the doorway for the enemy to enter into your life.

I remember how fearful I was before Jesus came into my life. Do you remember in your own life how fearful you were? Something I learned along the way was that sin opens up the door to fear. In Genesis 3:10 Adam says:

"...I heard the sound of Thee in the garden, and I was afraid because I was naked; so I hid myself."

Adam and Eve were in the garden, obeying God, and had dominion and authority. They had a great life. They had it made in the shade. Then they decided to disobey God, and eat from the tree in the middle of the garden, known as the tree of the knowledge of good and evil. When they disobeyed God suddenly they realized they were naked. They heard God coming and they went and hid themselves. They were afraid because of their sin.

Adam and Eve had a great life, but when they committed sin they became afraid. Sin opens the door to fear. Sin also makes you afraid of God, and causes you to stay away from church and the things of the Lord.

Anytime you willingly disobey God, you open the door to fear. I have never seen a person that did drugs who didn't have a great problem in the area of fear. The bottom line is this, sin is an open door for the enemy to come in. The enemy almost always uses fear to control you. To repent of your sins is the starting place to overcoming your fears.

Number Two: You have to face your fears. It doesn't matter how fear came into your life, simply be determined that it isn't going to rule you anymore.

The longer a fear has been in your life, the more difficult it will be to overcome it. It becomes a stronghold, a root. You have to be determined that it's not going to rule you or dominate you anymore. Fear isn't going to go away by ignoring it. If you don't face your fears, they will grow and eventually hold you hostage. Franklin D. Roosevelt said it this way: "You have nothing to fear but fear itself."

When an unhealthy fear is present in your life, you must know that God gave you three resources to overcome that fear. II Timothy 1:7 says, *For my God has not given me a spirit of fear, but of power, of love, and a sound mind.* God doesn't bring fear into your life. If it isn't God, then it must be the god of this world. God gave us His power, His love, and a sound and disciplined mind to overcome fear in this world.

We all face fears from time-to-time in our lives. Every person needs to examine their life, and make a determination to face their fears head-on so that they can overcome them. But remember, through His power you can do all things. We can overcome the fears that try to control us, because we can do all things through Christ that strengthens us.

In II Timothy 1:7, 'fear' actually translates as 'timidity.' In other words, my God has not given me a spirit of timidity. Fear makes you timid. The Bible says that the righteous shall be bold as lions. It doesn't say that the righteous shall be timid. It doesn't say that the righteous shall whine. It says that the righteous shall be bold as lions. The enemy wants you to walk in fear and timidity so he can control your future.

Timid people are always unsure of their decisions. They do very little for the Lord. They're afraid to do anything for God because of fear. Fear will always cause you to take your focus off of the Lord.

The enemy wants you to be unstable in your mind and unstable in your thinking. Fear starts in the mind. It's a real thing that permeates your entire body when it's there. Whatever your fears, you have to face them. You have to make up your mind to do the opposite of what fear is telling you to do. When fear tells you to run, you have to make up your mind that you're not going to run. Say what God says, "I can do all things through Christ." "Greater is He that's in me than he that's in the world." "I'll not fear what man can do to me." "Nothing shall separate me from the love of Christ."

I remember the very first time somebody asked me to do public speaking. I said, "No way, Jose! That's not for me!" I remember the Lord talking to me on the inside saying, "I want you to do this." I said, "No!" The Lord is gentle, patient, and kind. Over the weeks He kept talking to me, and I finally agreed to do it. There were only twenty-five people or so at that first meeting. I thought it was Madison Square Garden. My legs shook so badly, I was embarrassed watching my pants flap in the wind. I knew God was telling me to do this. I still didn't want to do it. I hated it. But I was faithful to do what God asked me to do. Over the years I have become more comfortable speaking in public, and here I am today, unafraid. There are times I still have butterflies in my stomach. You must face your fears. If you ever give in to your fears, you'll never become what God has called you to be.

The Lord showed me why I had the fear of public speaking. When I was eleven or twelve years old, my church asked me to quote a certain passage out of the Bible. I said I'd be happy to do it. I remember it was a big deal...there were many people there, even the pastor. I stood up to recite and forgot the passage. I did get through it, although the pastor had to get out his Bible and help me stumble through it. That was the point where the fear of public speaking was introduced into my life. That fear was introduced specifically to stop the call of God on my life.

Specific fears happen for specific reasons. Circumstances happen in young people's lives that can produce fear. It's nobody's fault. It just happens. If a water incident happened to you when you were young, you might be afraid of the water. I'm telling you right now, don't ever give in to that thing. Sign up for lessons at the YMCA. Make up your mind that fear is not going to control you. I don't care how old you are, make up your mind that God has not given you a spirit of fear and that you can do all things through Him. Face that fear, go after that thing, and don't quit until you have conquered it. Many people in life have been afraid of water and they didn't do anything about it. Then an incident occurred and they found themselves in deep water, fear overtook them, and they drowned. The fear that they had in their lives literally killed them.

Once you conquer a specific fear in your life, you get courageous. Soon you begin to overcome one area after another in which fear has held you captive. You begin to gain momentum, and then find yourself attacking every area in your life wherever fear is present. As you get some victories under your belt, watch what you can do through Jesus Christ.

There are many people today that are afraid of the Holy Spirit, because somewhere in their life somebody told them it was of the devil. Fear was introduced, but you can conquer that thing, just as you can conquer anything in Jesus' Name. Get into the Word. It is your blueprint for happiness and truth.

What about the fear of loving again? Everyone gets hurt. The devil will try to use fear to keep you isolated so you live a life of loneliness. That's a lie from the enemy.

It's very easy to overcome prejudice, which is nothing more than the fear of another race. Just start loving someone you're afraid of. It's the easiest thing in the world, like falling off a log. If you're afraid of black people, just start hugging them. You will say, I kind of like this. If you're afraid of white people, just start hugging them. You have to face your fears. You can't run from them. If you run from your fears, your fears will control you all the days of your life.

When I was a kid, I hated roller coasters. I made up my mind that I was going to face that fear. Not very long ago my wife and I drove out to an amusement park, and rode all three roller coasters, and then went home. Now I love roller coasters! I want to go out there again, just to ride the roller coasters, the ride I feared the most. When you get a victory under your belt, it gives you confidence.

Number Three: To overcome specific fears in your life, speak the Word of God out of your mouth.

Jesus always controlled the enemy with the Word. Not, "I bind you devil." He spoke the Word of God out of His mouth. You must remember that the Word of God is mighty and powerful, and sharper than a two-edged sword. The Word of

God will help you conquer whatever you're trying to overcome. Proverbs 18:21 says, **Death and life are in the power of the tongue.** Proverbs 6:2 says, **Don't be snared by the words of your mouth.** In other words, be careful what you say. Speak faith out of your mouth. Don't go around saying "I'm afraid, I'm afraid, I'm afraid."

If specific fears go unchallenged they will eventually control you and paralyze your life. Fear will make you feel like you live in a prison house. Jesus came to set you free. And the bottom line to all of it is this: If you don't face and conquer your fears, you will never become what God wants you to be. Every person should have a goal to defeat specific fears in their lives.

And on that day, when evening had come, Jesus said to them, "Let us go over to the other side." And leaving the multitude, they took Him along with them, just as He was, in the boat; and other boats were with Him. And there arose a fierce gale of wind, and the waves were breaking over the boat so much that the boat was already filling up. And He Himself was in the stern, asleep on a cushion; and they awoke Him and said unto Him, "Teacher, do you not care that we are perishing?" And being aroused, He rebuked the wind and said to the sea, "Be quiet and be still." And the wind died down and it became perfectly calm. And He said to them, "Why are you so fearful, how is it that you have no faith?"
Mark 4:35

The question is this: When the storms of life come, what do you do? Do you have faith in Him or do you panic? Do you throw up your hands and say, "Oh my God, why am I going through this?" Or do you say, "I trust you God. I know you love me. I know you have my best interests at heart. I trust you."

The disciples were saying here, "Hey Jesus, can't you see the waves going over the top of the boat? Don't you care about us? Have you forgotten us, Jesus, as we travel across the sea of life?" You can just see them now saying in undertones, "I thought you loved me Jesus. Don't you care enough to help us in the middle of the storm?" How many times in the middle of our storm do we say, "What's the matter God? I thought you loved me God. Why am I going through this, God?" But you see, Jesus was dealing here with a much more important issue. Jesus was saying that if you truly trust in God, there is no room for fear in your life. Are you trusting in God? Is there fear in your life?

If fear is operating, faith doesn't operate. The only way to conquer specific fears in your life is to get as close to Jesus as possible. Repent of your sins. Speak the Word of God out of your mouth. Face the fears that hold you captive, and be determined that you can do all things through Christ who strengthens you.

Chapter Six

God is My Refuge

God is our refuge and strength. A very present help in time of trouble. **Psalms 46:1**

We serve a God who is a big God. He is so big that He hung this world on nothing. He is so big that He has it all under control. Excuse my language, but <u>God ain't nervous</u>. I'm telling you right now there is nothing to fear. We serve a God that has it all under control. He knows the end from the beginning. And our God is our refuge and a very present help in time of trouble. He's the God of the now, not tomorrow, but today. He's the God of protection right now.

This world as you see it will pass away. I believe that the decade of the 90's will see the return of our Lord Jesus Christ. I believe that we are the generation that will see things get so bad that people will be running into the church of Jesus Christ because of fear in their lives.

Therefore we will not fear, though the earth should change, And though the mountains slip into the heart of the sea; Though its waters roar and foam, Though the mountains quake at its swelling pride. **Psalms 46:2-3**

God says that all things around us may stop. The mountains may fall flat to the ground. He's saying that this world is going to experience turmoil. But I know in whom I trust. His name is Jesus Christ.

Believe the Report of the Lord

Matthew 24 says that in the last days, times will grow worse. It says that people will be afraid for their lives and that times will grow so bad, that people will even ask to die because of the fear in their lives. I want you to know we live in a world that's afraid.

Being a believer in Jesus Christ doesn't stop the storms, but there is a place of safety in the rock of Christ Jesus. Though the storm may rage about me, He is the One that I run to. He is my ever-present help in time of trouble.

Did you know that growing up in Christ is a process? As we mature, we learn to trust the Lord, no matter what we see. We learn to go by the report of the Lord rather than the report of the world. But God has made a way through His Son, through the Blood of Christ. He has made a way of safety for you and it's through Jesus Christ our Lord and Savior.

As we mature, we learn to trust the Lord and we learn not to panic when difficult times come. Your brain is panic-prone and will tell you all kinds of foolish things. I want you to know that our God is so big and so magnificent that He will take what the enemy means to destroy us with and He'll turn it for our good. Jesus said, **"In this world you shall have tribulation."** But He also said, *"Be of good cheer, for I have already overcome the world."* The devil has already been defeated.

In Psalms 34:19 David said, *"Many are the afflictions of the righteous,"* or many are the difficulties or many are the problems of the righteous, *"but the Lord delivers him out of them all."*

Let me tell you something about the troubles and difficulties of this life. They always pass. God has a plan for you.

The first church of Jesus Christ, 2000 years ago, had a much different attitude about persecution than what we have today. Our attitude today is if things get a little bit rough, we just quit giving to God; if things get a little bit rough, we teach God a lesson, we won't come to church on Sunday. Somehow and some way we've got to get this persecution business straight. If you are living for God, it's going to cost you something. In Acts 5:41, the saints of old were rejoicing because God had considered them worthy to suffer persecution for His namesake. When persecution comes your way, God says to begin to rejoice because you are in the palm of His hand. The devil only persecutes those who are a threat to his kingdom. If the devil is leaving you alone, you are not worth much to the kingdom of God.

If you know who you are in Christ, if you are taking spiritual territory, the devil is terrified of you. He's running and he's bluffing along the way. The devil is full of hot air. He's a toothless lion. He is *as* a roaring lion. He's *not* a roaring lion. Two thousand years ago Jesus hung on the cross. He descended into the lower parts of the earth. He took our punishment upon Himself because we deserve to go to hell. He then arose victorious over death, over your enemy, over hell, and over the grave. When He came up out of that grave, He jerked the teeth out of that lion.

James 1:2 says, **Rejoice when persecution comes your way**. If persecution has come your way, it's because you've got the enemy on the run. The devil is trying to bluff you. Did you ever notice that if you make a stand for God, things get worse? It's just a bluff. Just hang in there with the report of the Lord, and it will change. The devil is all talk. He'll say, "I can defeat you,

I can defeat you," but he's nothing but hot air.

You Have God's Power

Nobody likes going through storms and tests and trials. But faith isn't faith until it's tested. "Oh yes, bless God, I have a lot of faith." You'll find out in the middle of a storm if you have faith or not. In Psalms 18 we see where King Saul had been chasing David for years trying to kill him. David's response was "The Lord is my Rock, He's my fortress, He's my deliverer, my God and my strength, my high tower and with His help I can crush a troop of soldiers, and I can leap over a wall." A Christian is not alone. He has the power of God on his side.

You see, through Christ you can do all things. The Lord is a high tower. He's a place of safety. That high tower is out of the enemy's reach. The storms may still come and blow, but you are out of the enemy's reach. Trouble can be on every side, but you must put your trust in Him.

We all have different ways we react when fear comes against our minds. I remember a period of time in my life when I went through "I bind you devil this, I bind you devil that, and the spirit of this, and the spirit of that." It can be heavy, trying to bind every devil. I learned something. You can do more to shake the devil's kingdom by praising God for five minutes than you can by binding the devil for an hour. When the difficult times come, throw your hands up high and just begin to praise Him; begin to worship Him; begin to glorify His name. Oh Lord, I praise you! Oh Lord, I praise you! Lord, I glorify your name! Hallelujah.

He who dwells in the shelter of the most high will abide in the shadow of the almighty. I will say to the Lord, my

refuge and my fortress, my God in whom I trust!
Psalms 91:1

I want you to know that if you are dwelling in the shelter of the Most High and if you are abiding in the shadow of the Almighty God, you can say, "Lord, You are my God, You are my fortress, You are my protection and in You I trust."

For it is He who delivers you from the snare of the trapper, and from the deadly pestilence....He will cover you with His wings and under His wings you may seek refuge. His faithfulness is a shield and a buckler. You will not be afraid of the terror by night, or the arrow that flies by day. **Psalms 91:3**

If you know your God, and in whom you trust, you can say with your own mouth "You are my God and my refuge." Let me also tell you this: You must be careful what you are saying with your mouth. Don't say, "I'm afraid of this and I'm afraid of that." Don't say, "I'm terrified of this and I'm terrified of that." Do what the Word of God says: "I say to my Lord, You are my refuge, You are my God in whom I will trust."

A thousand may fall at your side, and ten thousand at your right hand, but it shall not approach you....For you have made the Lord, my refuge, even the most High, your dwelling place. No evil will befall you, nor will any plague come near your tent. For He will give His angels charge concerning you, to guard you in all your ways. They will bear you up in their hands, lest you strike your foot against a stone. **Psalm 91:7 & 9**

Whether you're on your knees in Denver, Colorado, fighting for your family, or whether you've got a gun in your hand

and are at war, the Word of God says, "*Since God is your refuge, a thousand may fall at your side and ten thousand may fall at your right hand, but no evil shall come nigh you because He has His angels in charge over you to guard you, to protect you, to keep you safe lest you dash your foot against a stone."*

Place of Safety

If you're a Blood-bought believer in Jesus Christ, and if you're involved in sin...I don't mean just any little thing...I mean if there's a flagrant sin in your life and God's dealt with you on it, and you haven't done anything about it...if you are a believer and you allow that sin to stay, you are outside of His protection. You are outside of that place of refuge in your life.

I read a story not long ago about a man down in the Texas Gulf Coast. A hurricane was coming and he went into this shelter for protection...the hurricane came and the storm stopped. The people said, "Don't go outside, it may not be safe yet." But he was so curious about what was outside the walls of safety that he went outside believing the storm was over, but he had been in the eye of the hurricane. When the eye passed, the storm came once again. He was killed because he went out of that place of protection.

The devil wants you to be so curious about the world and what it has to offer that he lures you out of your place of safety. How do you react when the storms of life hit? What do you say about your God? I love the story about the three Hebrew children serving God. The king said bow or you'll burn. They said, "We're not going to compromise our lives. God is our refuge and in Him will we trust and He will protect us, and if He doesn't, we don't care because we're going to put our trust in Him." You know, of course, what happened in the midst of the fire...God delivered them.

Many times it looks as if our miracle has passed us by. The Word of God says even though it may appear as though all is lost, it's not over yet. When the bottom falls out in your life, your mind will tell you it's panic time. But as long as you serve the Lord Jesus Christ, you have no right to panic. He's always on time. He'll never be a minute early, but He'll never be a minute late. You see, everything is subject to change when you serve the King of Kings and the Lord of Lords. There is no need to worry over the world's situation. God has it all under control. Put it in God's hands. Trust Him and victory is going to come.

There is no need to pace the floor and lose sleep. Parents have a tendency to worry over their children. All their worrying will not change a thing. I tell you, get on your knees, begin to pray, ask God to send His angels of protection round about them, and go to bed and get some sleep. Cast your cares over on Him for He cares for you. That's what it says in 1 Peter 5:7: ***Cast all your care on Him, for He cares for you.*** Either you're carrying the burdens of your life, or He is. Either you've got these burdens strapped to your back, trying to get through life, or you're casting them over on Him. You've got a choice to make.

This world is dominated by fear. We as believers are not to allow the spirit of fear to control us. In Luke 21:10, Jesus speaks about things that are coming in the future, the end times, the last days.

And then He continued by saying to them "Nation will rise against nation, and kingdom against kingdom, and there will be great earthquakes." **Luke 21:10**

In the last 50 years, earthquakes have doubled every ten years. In the last 2 years, we have had earthquakes with the highest Richter scale measurements ever. Hurricanes have had the highest high pressures ever recorded in history in the last 2 years. The lowest low pressures have been recorded in the last year. This is just Bible prophesy being fulfilled in the last days. Luke 21:11-12 says:

And there will be great earthquakes, and in various places plagues and famines; and there will be terrors and great signs from heaven. But before all these things, they will lay their hands on you and will persecute you, delivering you to the synagogues and prisons, bringing you before kings and governors for My name's sake.

But then He says in verse 13, "But don't worry about it, chill out" because *it will lead to an opportunity for your testimony*. We can trust our God. He has it all under control. The final plan has already been laid down. It's going to be all right.

Men fainting from fear and the expectation of the things which are coming upon the world; for the powers of the heavens will be shaken. And then they will see the Son of Man coming in a cloud with power and great glory. But when these things begin to take place, straighten up and lift up your heads, because your redemption is drawing near. **Luke 21:26 - 28**

God's Word tells us that in the last days men and women will be so fearful that they will be dying from the fear in their lives. I believe that we have only seen the beginning of what Jesus referred to as the birth pangs. In other words, the earthquakes will increase and become greater. The hurricanes will increase and become greater. Signs to the world that God knows the end from the beginning. Signs to the world that Bible prophecies shall come to pass no matter who says they won't. Hearts will be fainting from fear.

Be on your guard that your hearts may not be weighted down with dissipation and drunkenness and the worries of life, and that day come on you suddenly like a trap.
Luke 21:34

He says, don't let the worries of this life get you down and don't get involved in drunkenness. He says that is dissipation and it goes by the wayside. Know that these are the last days and get serious with God.

The big guns of the devil are going to be squashed if you know about the Blood and the power of our Lord Jesus Christ. When the enemy comes in like a flood, God will raise up a standard against him. But you must know about the Blood. You've got to know about the power in Jesus' name. You've got to be committed to God. You've got to be in your place of safety.

The Last Days

We're living in a crucial time in history. We're living in what the Bible calls the last days. Some people even refer to us as the terminal generation. While the world is afraid of destruction, we are looking for the soon return of our Lord. You see, this world can fall apart around us and we have no right to fear. The worse it gets, the better it is for us. They can drop the bombs, but I know that my God is going to watch over me and take care of me.

Jesus said in Matthew 24:14 that when the Gospel is preached in all nations, then the end shall come. The gospel is going to be preached in Iraq. The gospel is going to be preached in Israel. The gospel is going to be preached in Pakistan and in China. The gospel is going to be preached in all nations and then the end shall come. Revelation 12 says the devil will do his handiwork in a powerful way in the last days, knowing that he has only a short time left.

You see, the enemy wants you to be afraid so he can control your life. He wants you to think this world's falling apart, but I want you to know that God has it all under control. We are nearing the end. Jesus is coming soon...a year, 10 years, I don't know...but I know He's coming soon. No matter what happens, I can say "in God I have put my trust." No matter what happens, I can say, "I will not fear what man can do to me." You see, this world is in trouble. But I serve a God who turns impossible situations around.

I know that God is working a plan in my life. I don't go by what I see. We must believe the report of the Lord, not the report of this world. If you know Jesus, you don't have to be afraid. Bible prophecy shall be fulfilled in these last days. Times will grow more difficult, but you can have peace in the middle of the storm.

Jesus is coming for His bride. Are you ready? Ready or not, He's coming. This world is living in much fear and trembling, but there is a place of safety for all who call on His name, the name of the Lord Jesus Christ. I've read the end of God's Book. We win. The devil loses. Are you on the winning side?

You must determine in your heart today that you will no longer live in fear. Our enemy, the devil, can no longer steal your joy or your peace. It's all a matter of choice. If you want to be free from the fears and cares of this world, I invite you to take a moment and pray.

PRAYER

I desire, Father, to go into my Promised Land. I desire the Good News to take me to victory. I will change my words. I will not say what the enemy wants me to say. I will say what the Word of God says. I make a choice today to serve Jesus Christ, to turn my back on this world. I am sorry, Lord, for any wrongs that I have done. Show me how to turn it around. Thank You, Father, that You are not mad at me. I make a decision to have an overcoming attitude, not a grasshopper mentality. I may have been beaten down in my past, but I can rise above my past, because Jesus lives in me. I can overcome because greater is He who lives in me than he that lives in the world. I make a choice today to forgive all those in my past that have hurt me or beaten me down. I do it by faith, and as a choice. My life will never be the same, in Jesus' Name. I turn my burdens, fears, and worries over to You. I do it by faith, and as a choice. Thank You, Lord, that I have refuge and peace in You. My life will never be the same, in Jesus' name.

Books and Cassette Tape Available

The Blood of Jesus	4 Pack	$12.00
Bring On The Joy	4 Pack	12.00
Finances	3 Pack	9.00
Forgiveness	4 Pack	12.00
Grace	6 Pack	18.00
Growing Up In Christ	6 Pack	18.00
Healing	6 Pack	18.00
The Holy Spirit	6 Pack	18.00
Jesus	6 Pack	18.00
The Last Days	6 Pack	18.00
Love	6 Pack	18.00
Marriage and The Family	6 Pack	18.00
Mountain Moving Faith	6 Pack	18.00
Overcoming Depression	4 Pack	12.00
Pride	4 Pack	12.00
Prayer	4 Pack	12.00
Rejection	4 Pack	12.00
Worry	4 Pack	12.00
Salvation	4 Pack	12.00
Sex	4 Pack	12.00
Spiritual Warfare	4 Pack	12.00

Books

If God Can Forgive You, You Can Forgive Yourself	$ 5.00
Overcoming Depression	5.00

(Tapes and Books-Postage and Handling Included)

Master Card and Visa orders are welcome.

If you wish to purchase any of Pastor Dennis Leonard's teaching materials please place your order by writing or calling Dennis Leonard Publications at the location listed below.

Dennis Leonard Publications
1301 South Clinton Street
Denver, Colorado 80231
(303) 369-8514